Author: Lan Donne

ISBN HARDBACK: 978-9908-52-020-9

ISBN PAPERBACK: 978-9908-52-021-6

ISBN EBOOK: 978-9908-52-022-3

Enchanted Snowfall

Softly it falls, a quiet grace,
Whispers of winter, a tender embrace.
Blankets of white on the slumbering ground,
Magic awakens where silence is found.

Twinkling like gems in the pale moonlight,
Dancing with shadows, a mystical sight.
Nature's own canvas, pure and serene,
A world transformed, like a beautiful dream.

Chilled Stars

In the stillness of night, they sparkle bright,
Chilled stars twinkle with ethereal light.
Whispers of cosmos in the chilly air,
A symphony played by the universe's flare.

Each twinkle a promise, a tale to unfold,
Ancient and wise, with secrets untold.
Guiding the weary with shimmering beams,
Holding the magic of countless dreams.

Brilliant Shard

A brilliant shard from the depths of night,
Catching the echoes of sparkling light.
It dances on edges, so sharp, so clear,
Reflecting the wonders that whisper near.

Emeralds and rubies in colors that gleam,
A prism of thoughts, a daydreamer's dream.
Each facet a moment, each shine a desire,
A treasure discovered, igniting the fire.

Diamond Dust

Falling like dreams from the heavens above,
Sprinkles of magic, like whispers of love.
Diamond dust glistens, enchanting the night,
Wrapping the world in a cocoon of light.

Soft as the sigh of the winter's breath,
Inviting the warmth in the chill of death.
Glimmers of hope in a frozen embrace,
A shimmering promise of beauty and grace.

Ethereal Glimmer

In twilight's embrace, stars gently gleam,
A dance of light in a silver dream.
Whispers of hope in the cool night air,
Painting a canvas, beyond compare.

Veils of dazzle stretch across the sky,
With secrets of ages, as time drifts by.
Moonbeams cascading on waves so bright,
A soft serenade, in the depths of night.

Icebound Wonders

Frozen rivers weave through the land,
Nature's own sculptures, carefully planned.
Crystal formations rise to the light,
Each shard a story, a marvel of night.

Snowflakes in silence, they twirl and spin,
A ballet of winter, where dreams begin.
Icicles glisten on branches so bare,
A wonderland waiting for hearts that dare.

Faint Flickers of Winter

Soft embers flicker in the hearth's warm glow,
While outside the world coats itself in snow.
Chill in the air, yet warmth in our souls,
As we gather close, sharing our roles.

Whispers of frost paint the windows bright,
Each crystalline pattern a dance of light.
Laughter echoes in the still, cool night,
Joyful moments embraced, pure delight.

Whispering Crystals

Gentle winds carry secrets untold,
Crystals that shimmer, a sight to behold.
Frost-kissed petals in morning's first beam,
Nature's own magic, a soft, fleeting dream.

Each droplet glistens like stars in the dawn,
A symphony played on the lawns, now drawn.
Echoes of beauty in silence resound,
In every moment, pure wonder is found.

Chilled Radiant Dreams

In the still night, whispers hum,
Stars above, a soft drum.
Moonlight dances on silent streams,
Embracing the chilled radiant dreams.

Breezes carry tales of yore,
Through the branches, they explore.
Each leaf glimmers, shimmering beams,
Awakening the chilled radiant dreams.

Frosted fields, a blanket white,
Capturing the fleeting light.
With every step, the heart redeems,
Finding peace in chilled radiant dreams.

Laughter echoes, spirits soar,
Moments cherished, never bore.
In laughter's glow, joy redeems,
Wrapped warmly in chilled radiant dreams.

As dawn breaks, colors gleam,
Life awakens from the dream.
Yet in the morn, one still gleams,
Carrying forth, chilled radiant dreams.

Luminous Chill

The moonlight softly glows,
In the air, a quiet freeze.
Stars twinkle in repose,
Nature whispers through the trees.

Frost clings to every branch,
A shimmer upon the ground.
Silence forms a gentle dance,
As night wraps the world around.

Snowflakes drift from the sky,
Each one a fleeting dream.
Winter's breath is a sigh,
In the heart, a calm stream.

Crunching steps in the dark,
Echoes of a frosty night.
Silent paths leave their mark,
Beneath the soft silver light.

With every breath, a cloud,
Mist rising with the breath.
Wrapped in this quiet shroud,
Life pauses without death.

Winter's Gleam

Morning sun spills its gold,
On the blanket of pure white.
Stories of winter told,
In the chill of fading light.

Glistening on the trees,
Branches wear a crown of ice.
Every whisper of the breeze,
Bears the chill of soft advice.

A world in quiet grace,
With each step, a dream unfolds.
Nature's calm, a warm embrace,
In the air, a promise holds.

Twilight casts a spell,
As shadows stretch and blend.
Winter's magic, we can tell,
In the dusk, time seems to bend.

Stars hang like glowing charms,
In the velvet skies above.
Winter's eve in arms,
Wraps us in its frosty love.

Celestial Sparkle

Stars adorn the night's dark veil,
A symphony of distant light.
In this hush, tales set sail,
Across the canvas of the night.

Comets streak like whispers fast,
Crossing paths in darkened skies.
A fleeting moment, vast,
Fleeting dreams that dance and rise.

Galaxies spin in silent grace,
Cradling wonders far from sight.
In this magical embrace,
The universe ignites the night.

Moonbeams weave a silver thread,
Through the branches, soft and wise.
Guiding hopes as words are said,
In shadows, ancient lullabies.

Cosmic winds softly blow,
Carrying secrets, tales untold.
In their breath, the stars all glow,
A celestial wonder to behold.

Crystal Mists

Morning shimmers with fresh dew,
A mist blankets the waking dawn.
Whispers soft as the sky turns blue,
In the silence, dreams are drawn.

Shadows dance on fields so wide,
Nature breathes a gentle sigh.
In this world, time does abide,
As fleeting moments softly fly.

Lakes reflect a soft embrace,
Mirror worlds in stillness found.
Every ripple leaves a trace,
Of secrets kept beneath the ground.

Misty paths lead hearts to roam,
Through the quiet woods they weave.
In each step, a sense of home,
In the air, the magic leaves.

Evening falls with a touch of grace,
Stars awaken in the night.
Crystal mists begin to chase,
The lingering warmth of fading light.

Crystalized Echoes

In the silence of the night,
Whispers of frost take flight.
Glistening on the ground,
A beauty profound.

Every breath forms a ghost,
Memories tight, we hold close.
Echoes of laughter ring,
In winter's embrace, we cling.

Moonlight dances on the trees,
Carrying the winter breeze.
Crystal shards catch the glow,
Of dreams we used to sow.

In the chill, hearts align,
Among the stars, we define.
Paths crossed on nights like this,
In the frost, we find bliss.

To the rhythm of snowflakes fall,
Nature's canvas, a white pall.
Each layer tells a tale,
In silence, we unveil.

Shining Frost

Dewdrops glisten in the dawn,
As the sun begins to yawn.
Frosty patterns crisp and bright,
Adorn the world with pure delight.

A silver veil, the ground does wear,
Nature's secret, light and rare.
Branches clothed in shimmering lace,
Reflecting winter's soft embrace.

Windswept fields of crystal white,
In the stillness, pure and right.
Echoes linger, soft and sweet,
Where cold and warmth gently meet.

Every step a fleeting sound,
As I tread on frozen ground.
Shining frost beneath my feet,
Whispers of the winter's beat.

Evening falls, the sky ignites,
Stars awaken, twinkling lights.
In the quiet, spirits bloom,
Beneath the frost, life finds room.

Winter's Lament

Branches bare and shadows long,
Echoes of a lost song.
Winter sighs, a gentle breath,
Whispers of fleeting death.

Footprints fade, erased by time,
Memories in frozen rhyme.
Every silence tells a tale,
In the snow, our hopes set sail.

Frigid winds, they howl and moan,
In the midst, we're not alone.
Together we face the cold,
In our hearts, warmth to hold.

Dreams wrapped in scarves so tight,
Guiding us through endless night.
Though the world may seem so bare,
Love's embrace is always there.

As the seasons shift and change,
We learn to adapt, to rearrange.
Winter's lament softly fades,
In spring's warmth, the heart invades.

Radiant Winter Nights

Underneath the starry veil,
Silent whispers tell their tale.
Radiance in the frosty air,
Enchantments linger everywhere.

The moon hangs low, a silver glow,
Painting dreams on sheets of snow.
Each twinkle a story told,
In the chill, our hopes unfold.

Wrapped in melodies of night,
The world sparkles, pure delight.
Candles flicker, casting light,
In the depths of winter's bite.

Gathered warmth around the fire,
Hearts ablaze with sweet desire.
Through the cold, together we soar,
In winter nights, forevermore.

The frost creates a wondrous scene,
As dreams glimmer, calm and serene.
Radiant nights, we hold them dear,
In our hearts, winter's cheer.

Radiance of the Freeze

In winter's breath, the world is still,
A frozen canvas, white and chill.
Stars above begin to gleam,
In her light, all shadows dream.

Beneath a cloak of crystal white,
The trees stand tall, in pure delight.
Moonlight dances on the snow,
A serene glow, a gentle flow.

Frosted branches, kissed by night,
Reflecting dreams, a soft twilight.
Echoes of a silent night,
Wrapped in warmth, devoid of fright.

The air is crisp, a peaceful song,
In this stillness, we belong.
Nature whispers, soft and low,
In the heart of winter's glow.

As dawn arrives, the colors rise,
A palette painted in the skies.
Radiant beauty, pure and bright,
In the freeze, we find our light.

Crystal Cascade

Waterfalls of winter's grace,
Cascading down in a frosty race.
Each drop a gem in sunlight's beam,
A crystal dance, a flowing dream.

Over rocks, with gleeful cheer,
They tumble forth, so pure, so clear.
In swirling mists, the rainbows play,
Nature's art in a wild display.

Beneath the surface, whispers creep,
Secrets of the cold, they keep.
The sound of water sings its tune,
In harmony with the silver moon.

Surrounded by the frozen trees,
The air is filled with gentle breeze.
Each swirl and splash, a fleeting sight,
Captured in the spectrum's light.

As winter wanes, the cascade flows,
With thawing warmth, the river knows.
In every drop, a story told,
Of nature's beauty, bright and bold.

Frosted Whispers

A tranquil hush, the world asleep,
In frosted dreams, the shadows creep.
Whispers of the night unfold,
Tales of winter, soft and cold.

Silvery flakes drift down like lace,
Covering all in a gentle embrace.
Silence reigns, the stars align,
In this moment, the world is divine.

Pine trees wear a snowy crown,
Amidst the stillness, not a sound.
Frosty whispers brush the air,
Nature's breath, a wintry prayer.

Beneath the moon, a secret dance,
In shadows deep, we find our chance.
Each glimmer, a fleeting glance,
Of frosted realms, a timeless stance.

As dawn breaks, the whispers fade,
In sunlight's warmth, the frost is laid.
A new day blooms with vibrant hues,
Yet frosted whispers still ensue.

Shimmering Mortal

In twilight's grasp, we find our place,
A shimmering moment, a fleeting grace.
Life flickers in the fading light,
A dance of shadows, day to night.

Human hearts, both frail and bold,
Chasing dreams, their stories told.
In glimmers, we embrace the fight,
Amidst the dark, we seek the bright.

Each laugh and tear, a whispered thread,
In shimmering tapestries, we're led.
Through trials faced, we find our way,
In every struggle, come what may.

Ephemeral joys and sorrows blend,
In life's mosaic, we transcend.
A spark ignites in the mortal scheme,
Reflecting life, a wondrous dream.

As stars twinkle in the vast expanse,
We hold our hopes, we take the chance.
In shimmering moments, we collide,
Embracing the mortal, side by side.

Sparkling Silence

In the hush of night, stars gleam bright,
Whispers of dreams take graceful flight.
The world slumbers soft, wrapped in calm,
A tranquil embrace, a soothing balm.

Shadows dance gently, under pale moon,
Each breath is a secret, a tender tune.
Echoes of silence, a sweet refrain,
Cradled in twilight, free from pain.

Rustling leaves weave a tale of still,
Nature's quietude, a heart to fill.
The air, crisp and clear, a moment to hold,
In sparkling silence, stories unfold.

Luminous Frost

Morning dew glistens, a pearl-like sheen,
Nature's canvas painted, vibrant and clean.
A whisper of chill, a blanket of white,
Luminous frost, in the soft morning light.

Trees stand adorned in shimmering lace,
Each branch a spell in winter's embrace.
Sunrise breaks softly, a golden crown,
Kissing the frost, turning silver to brown.

Footsteps crunch on a path not yet trod,
In this frozen realm, I walk with God.
A world transformed in stillness divine,
Luminous frost, in silence, we shine.

Ethereal Ice

A crystal world, vast and serene,
Ethereal ice, like a delicate dream.
Mirrored reflections, a dance of light,
In glacial whispers, day turns to night.

Frozen cascades, a shimmering veil,
Nature's pure artistry, a haunting tale.
Through chilly corridors, spirits glide,
In the heart of winter, secrets reside.

Each flake a wonder, a fleeting grace,
In this fragile beauty, we find our place.
Ethereal ice, a world that gleams,
A frozen whisper, unspoken dreams.

Crystalized Dreams

In the still of the night, dreams take flight,
Crystalized visions, shimmering bright.
They dance through the ether, light as air,
Whispers of hope in the moonlight's glare.

Each dream a jewel, a story untold,
Wrapped in the night like treasures of gold.
They twirl like leaves in a gentle breeze,
In the glow of the stars, hearts find their ease.

Beneath the vast sky, they wander free,
Crystalized dreams, a sweet reverie.
In soft solitude, they bravely gleam,
A testament to life, each fleeting dream.

Snowy Reflections

Whispers of snow fall slow,
Covering the earth below.
Silent night, a calming grace,
Nature's quilt, a soft embrace.

Moonlight glimmers on the ground,
In the stillness, peace is found.
Stars reflect in purest white,
Guiding dreams through winter's night.

Footprints left in deep drifts lie,
Stories told as time goes by.
Memories wrapped in chilly air,
Love and warmth beyond compare.

A frosty breath, the world asleep,
Into the depths, the stillness creeps.
Every flake a tale to share,
In the silence, beauty rare.

Snowy reflections, soft and bright,
Painting moments, pure delight.
In this season, hearts unite,
Underneath the winter's light.

Diamond Fragments

Twinkling gems on frozen ground,
Nature's treasures all around.
Sunlight dances, magic gleams,
In the frost, we find our dreams.

Every flake a prism's glow,
Casting rainbows in the snow.
Fragile beauty, fleeting grace,
Captured light in time and space.

Crystal whispers, secrets held,
In the chill, our hearts are swelled.
Each moment shines, a fleeting breath,
Life reflected in the depth.

As the chill wraps 'round our soul,
In these fragments, we are whole.
Finding joy in icy streams,
In diamond fragments, lost in dreams.

Glistening worlds where shadows play,
In the light, the dark gives way.
Every sparkle tells a tale,
In this wonder, we prevail.

Enchanted Ice

Beneath the moon, a shimmer bright,
Wonders born from chilly night.
Frosted branches touch the air,
In this magic, dreams to share.

Glistening paths of crystal lace,
Nature's art, a bold embrace.
In the silence, voices rise,
Echoes dance beneath the skies.

Frozen lakes with stories deep,
Mirrored worlds that gently sleep.
Every glint, a whispered song,
In this realm, we all belong.

Whirls of snowflakes, soft as sighs,
Fluttering where the winter lies.
In enchanted ice, we see
A reflection of you and me.

Through the cold, our hearts ignite,
Finding warmth in shared delight.
In the chill, our spirits sway,
In enchanted ice, let's stay.

Frosted Luminescence

Radiant glow upon the frost,
In the beauty, never lost.
Whispers of the chilly air,
Frosted luminescence rare.

Subtle sparkles in the night,
Stars above in purest light.
Every shimmer, magic weaves,
In the stillness, our heart believes.

Winter's breath, a painting clear,
Softly drawing you near.
Moments of ephemeral bliss,
In the frost, a precious kiss.

Gentle touch of icy grace,
In the landscape, we embrace.
Every glimmer holds a dream,
In this world, we softly beam.

Frosted light, a guiding star,
Leading us, no matter how far.
In each glow, a love we share,
In frosted luminescence, we care.

Shimmering Shards

In the twilight's gentle breeze,
Shards of light dance on the ground,
Colors break and gently tease,
Whispers of beauty all around.

Mirrors of dreams in the air,
Reflecting hopes that softly gleam,
Fragments caught in moments rare,
A canvas of a silent dream.

Glimmers trace the edges bright,
Gliding like a fleeting thought,
Casting magic, pure delight,
In every sparkle, wisdom sought.

They whisper secrets of the sky,
Each glint a story yet untold,
In their shimmer, we learn to fly,
Embracing warmth in the cold.

With glittering shards, hopes resound,
Every sparkle sings its tune,
In the twilight, beauty found,
A timeless hymn beneath the moon.

Twinkling Haze

In the dark, a soft embrace,
Twinkling sparks begin to rise,
Filling spaces, leaving trace,
In the haze, a world complies.

A mystical, enchanting fog,
Glimmers dance in muted light,
Softly weaving through the slog,
Giving day a touch of night.

Stars awaken in the mist,
Whispers carried on the breeze,
Every twinkle, love unkissed,
Swaying gently through the trees.

In the twilight's gentle fold,
Magic lingers, dreams take flight,
Stories waiting to be told,
Shining softly, pure and bright.

Twinkling haze, you weave delight,
In your grasp, the heart will sway,
Through the dark, you bring the light,
Guiding souls along the way.

Silvered Ice

Underneath a chilling veil,
Silvered whispers spread their wings,
Each reflection tells a tale,
Of winter's grasp and quiet things.

Frozen dreams in crystal lace,
Shimmering like stars at dawn,
Every thought a sacred space,
In the silence, life goes on.

Glistening paths of purest white,
Footprints lost in morning's glow,
Nature's canvas, a breath of light,
Every stroke, a tale of snow.

Silvered ice, a world confined,
With beauty caught in frosted time,
Each edge sharp, yet intertwined,
Nature's song in chimes that rhyme.

In the heart of winter's grasp,
Silvered ice, a fleeting sight,
In every crack, a gentle rasp,
Whispering tales of pure delight.

Chilling Brilliance

In the stillness of the night,
Chilling brilliance takes its hold,
Stars above shine ever bright,
Glistening with a heart so bold.

Fragments spark in icy air,
Each flicker, a breath of bold,
Whispers drifting everywhere,
Stories of the young and old.

Luminous and cold embrace,
Illuminating shadows deep,
In the silence, find your place,
Where the heart can learn to leap.

Underneath the velvet sky,
Chilling brilliance hums its tune,
As the moments pass us by,
Beneath the gently smiling moon.

With each twinkle, we find peace,
Chilling brilliance warms the night,
In its glow, our souls release,
In that calm, we feel the light.

Icy Stardust

In the night sky, glimmers gleam,
Icy stardust dances, a dream.
Whispers of cold in the moonlight,
Shimmering sparks, ever so bright.

They twinkle softly, in silence vast,
Moments frozen, shadows cast.
A canvas of blue, touched by frost,
Each shimmering light, never lost.

Breathe in the chill, feel the glow,
Wonders of winter, a magical show.
Glistening jewels on midnight's cloak,
Wrapped in a blanket of fog and smoke.

Frosted petals on the ground,
In this beauty, peace is found.
Tonight, the cosmos together weave,
A taste of magic, we believe.

Icy stardust, a spell it weaves,
A tapestry where the heart believes.
Beneath the stars, in quiet streams,
We walk in wonder, holding dreams.

Gleaming Frozen Essence

Crystal leaves in the morning light,
Gleaming frost, a breathtaking sight.
Nature's art, painted with care,
Whispers of winter hang in the air.

Each breath crystallizes, hangs undone,
In the crisp dawn, a world begun.
Frozen essence, a treasure kept,
In the stillness, where silence wept.

Sparkling rivers, glacial and free,
Reflecting shards of eternity.
Every moment, a tale to tell,
In the heart's silence, memories swell.

With the sun's rise, the frost retreats,
Nature's rhythm, a dance that beats.
Still, it lingers, inside our hearts,
Gleaming frozen, where magic starts.

Through the branches, soft light glows,
Painting shadows with soft, bright throws.
In this essence, we find our way,
Gleaming beauty, in night and day.

Moonlit Frost

Under the moon, the night unfolds,
Frost blankets dreams in silver holds.
Whispering winds, a soft embrace,
In moonlit magic, we find our place.

Stars twinkle down in the crisp air,
Frosty edges, a world so rare.
Shadows dance under the pale light,
Moonlit frost, a beautiful sight.

Each step forward, crunch and crack,
In the stillness, we can't look back.
Glittering pathways, so serene,
Guided by moonbeams, a gentle sheen.

As daylight wanes, the chill stays near,
In this wonder, there's nothing to fear.
Bound by the light, enveloped in peace,
In moonlit frost, all worries cease.

Together we wander, hand in hand,
Across this frozen, enchanted land.
With every breath, a moment to pause,
In the moonlight's glow, we find our cause.

Shards of Light

In the stillness, fragments gleam,
Shards of light, a radiant beam.
Scattered across the crystal floor,
Whispers of hope, forevermore.

Each ray dances, a flicker divine,
Illuminating paths that intertwine.
A kaleidoscope of dreams takes flight,
In the heart of darkness, love ignites.

Reflections shimmer, bright and bold,
Each shard a story waiting to unfold.
Connected moments, tender and bright,
Guided by echoes of pure delight.

As twilight fades, the stars align,
Shards of light in harmony shine.
In the gathering fog, we hold our breath,
Celebrating life, in the face of death.

Through the night, let kindness flow,
In each shard, let compassion grow.
With tender hearts, we learn to see,
In the darkness, we find unity.

Radiant Snowfall

Softly landing, pure and bright,
Whispers dance in the moonlight.
Nature's quilt, a gentle sigh,
Blankets earth as dreams drift by.

Trees adorned in sparkling white,
Kissing branches in the night.
Silent symphonies unfold,
Magic stories, silent, told.

Children laughing, snowflakes swirl,
Winter's joy, a joyous whirl.
Footprints trace a frosty path,
Echoes of the season's laugh.

Frosty breath upon the air,
With each step, a world laid bare.
Crystals twinkle, glisten bright,
In the quiet of the night.

As the sunrise paints the skies,
Radiance breaks, the cold complies.
Each flake glows, a sapphire gem,
In winter's grasp, we find our hem.

Frosted Elegance

In the stillness, beauty calls,
Winter's grace in gentle falls.
Glistening pearls on every branch,
Nature's art, a silent dance.

Veils of frost on rooftops lie,
Whispers of the cold night sky.
Each breath mingles, soft and sweet,
With every heartbeat, winter greets.

Echoes of a crystal chime,
Fleeting moments, frozen time.
As the world wears white attire,
Hearts ignite with warm desire.

Fluttering flurries swirl and play,
Quiet secrets of the day.
In each shimmer, elegance glows,
A tranquil beauty that bestows.

Lace-like patterns on the pane,
Promises of soft refrain.
Frosted whispers fill the air,
In this elegance, we share.

Ethereal Shimmer

Moonbeams kiss the snowy ground,
In stillness, peace is found.
Shadows dance beneath the stars,
World transformed, forgetting scars.

Glimmers rise as spirits soar,
Whispers carried from afar.
Draped in silver, night unfolds,
Stories whispered, secrets told.

Laughing echoes on the breeze,
As joy lingers in the trees.
Frosty fingers touch the night,
Crafting beauty, pure delight.

Each flake holds a world within,
Ethereal dreams begin to spin.
In their twirl, we find our place,
A moment's pause, a warm embrace.

Veils of magic softly swirled,
Hearts enchanted, thoughts unfurled.
In this glimmer, dreams take flight,
Chasing sparks in the quiet night.

Glinting Chill

As twilight beckons, shadows creep,
In the hush, the world's asleep.
Glinting crystals catch the glow,
Whispers of the winds that blow.

In icy breath, secrets lie,
Frosty gleam in the night sky.
Every corner, every street,
Wrapped in silk, a pure retreat.

Footfalls echo, sharp and clear,
In the chill, there's naught to fear.
Moonlight dances upon the snow,
Guiding hearts where dreams can flow.

Each breath frosts the air around,
Nature's beauty, lost and found.
In the quiet, souls take flight,
Cradled softly by the night.

Glinting chill on winter's breath,
Nature whispers of love and death.
In every twinkle, life returns,
For in cold warmth, the heart yearns.

Glacial Gleam

In the stillness of the night,
Shimmering ice takes flight.
Moonlight dances on the lake,
A silent breath, a gentle wake.

Crystal shards in the air,
Frosty whispers without a care.
A breath of winter's magic call,
Nature's beauty, embracing all.

Icicles hang, sharp and bright,
Reflecting the stars, a breathtaking sight.
Glistening paths where shadows play,
Under the hush of the frosty day.

Bridges weave through snow and ice,
As winter's wonder pays the price.
Every step, a spark of glee,
In this realm of mystery.

Voices echo, soft and clear,
As shimmering dreams draw near.
In this world of glacial grace,
We find our peace, we find our place.

Luminous Winter

Snowflakes fall like whispered dreams,
Blanketing the world in silver beams.
The chilly air, a tempting sigh,
Beneath the vast and starry sky.

Pine trees wear their coats of white,
Boughs bending low, a wondrous sight.
Fires crackle as shadows sway,
In the glow of this winter's play.

Luminous night with a frosty breath,
Tells the tales of life and death.
In each flake, a story lies,
A dance of time beneath the skies.

Quiet is the world outside,
Where all of nature seems to hide.
Yet in the silence, life does hum,
In luminous whispers, spring will come.

As dawn breaks with hues so warm,
Winter's chill begins to transform.
Golden rays on soft white ground,
A beauty in silence, profoundly profound.

Frigid Sparkle

Underneath the icy veil,
Whispers drift like a ghostly trail.
Stars reflecting, a timeless grace,
In the quiet of this frozen space.

Branches draped in crystalline lace,
A fairy tale in every place.
The air is sharp, yet sweetly pure,
In this mystery, we endure.

Footprints mark the snowy floor,
Leading to dreams forevermore.
Frigid sparkle in each breath,
Reminds us of the cycle of death.

Frozen lakes, a glassy sheen,
A canvas for the woods' serene.
Nature whispers in every hue,
Frigid delights, both old and new.

In the depths of winter's hold,
Beauty shines like liquid gold.
A frigid heart, yet warm within,
A dance where the story begins.

Dazzling Frostbite

A crispness dances through the air,
Frostbite sparkles everywhere.
Edges painted with icy sheen,
A dazzling world, divinely clean.

Winter's breath upon my face,
Chilling whispers, a fierce embrace.
Each moment lingers with delight,
In the wonder of this starry night.

Colors fade to shades of gray,
Yet beauty finds its bold display.
Glistening paths beneath our feet,
Nature's harmony feels so sweet.

With every breath, a plume of mist,
In the silence, we coexist.
Frostbite stings, but souls ignite,
In this sparkling, wintry night.

The world asleep, yet alive with light,
Dazzling dreams set to take flight.
With every turn, our hearts may race,
In winter's arms, we find our place.

Frosted Reflections

A mirror of ice, so bright,
It glimmers in the dawn's light.
Each crystal holds a fleeting thought,
In silence, frozen dreams are caught.

The world outside is hushed and still,
Nature wrapped in winter's chill.
Every breath a cloud of white,
In this moment, pure delight.

Trees wear coats of sparkling white,
Branches bow with purest light.
Footprints trace a path so clear,
In this frost, I draw you near.

Whispers dance on frosted air,
Echoes of a whispered prayer.
The sun will rise, the thaw will start,
But on this ice, you hold my heart.

The evening falls with shadows deep,
A blanket over dreams we keep.
Frosted reflections, a transient scene,
Carved in silence, ever serene.

Luminous Solitude

In the stillness of the night,
Stars weave tales in silver light.
Moonbeams dance on barren ground,
In this solitude, peace is found.

A single lantern flickers bright,
Guiding thoughts in endless flight.
Whispers flow like gentle streams,
In the silence, cradle dreams.

Each shadow tells a story rare,
Of quiet moments, hearts laid bare.
Lonely echoes softly sway,
In luminous hues of fading day.

The world outside is lost in sleep,
In solitude, my secrets keep.
Radiant thoughts in gentle flow,
As starry skies begin to glow.

I find solace in the dark,
A spark ignites, ignites a spark.
Luminous solitude, my guide,
In this embrace, I confide.

Fluorescent Freeze

Colors burst in vivid light,
A canvas painted bright and white.
Every flake a frozen thrill,
In the glow, time stands still.

Neon streaks across the night,
Fluorescent dreams take their flight.
Each moment bursts like fireworks,
In this vibrant world, joy lurks.

Twinkling lights on frosted trees,
Whispers carried by the breeze.
Frozen laughter fills the air,
A symphony beyond compare.

In this chill where brightness gleams,
Each heartbeat echoes vivid dreams.
Fluorescent freeze, a surreal play,
In the magic of this day.

As the dawn begins to break,
Splashing color in its wake.
A vibrant blend of dusk and dawn,
In this freeze, my spirit's drawn.

A Chill of Radiance

In the twilight, shadows creep,
A chill of radiance, soft and deep.
Stars awaken, bright and bold,
Whispers carried on the cold.

Frost blankets the world outside,
An ethereal glow, a quiet pride.
Each twinkle sings a lullaby,
Beneath the vast and starry sky.

The night exhales a silent dream,
In silver tides, we flow like streams.
A chill of radiance in the air,
Wrapped in warmth, we shed our care.

Every heartbeat, a firefly,
Drifting through the endless sky.
Within this calm, my heart takes flight,
In the tender glow of night.

As dawn approaches, weary and thin,
The chill recedes, the day begins.
But in my heart, the light remains,
A chill of radiance, love sustains.

Icy Elegance

In the quiet hush of dusk,
Glistening pavements shine bright,
Snowflakes dance in soft whispers,
A world wrapped in pure white.

Branches wear coats of glitter,
Crystal jewels on every tip,
Nature's art, a silent splendor,
As frozen dreams begin to slip.

Moonlight bathes the landscape,
Casting shadows, long and lean,
Frosty breath on chilled glass,
A serene and tranquil scene.

Footprints mark a fleeting journey,
In a tale that won't last long,
As the icy breath of winter,
Sings its softly woven song.

Time stands still, a precious moment,
Where the seasons briefly meet,
In the icy grasp of elegance,
Winter paints a world complete.

Celestial Frost

Stars twinkle in a velvet sky,
While frost decorates the earth,
Every breath a cloud of wonder,
A glimpse of beauty, a quiet birth.

Crystalline paths in soft moonlight,
Mark the way through snowy fields,
Whispers echo in the stillness,
A gentle touch, the night yields.

Pines stand tall in silent reverence,
Their boughs heavy with white lace,
As the world glows in quiet magic,
Embracing winter's sweet embrace.

Each moment gleams with a shimmer,
Time slows down, then takes a breath,
A ballet framed in frosty stillness,
Where the dance of life meets death.

As dawn breaks on the horizon,
Colors clash in soft retreat,
Celestial frost shall linger,
In our hearts, forever sweet.

Twinkling Winter Nights

Underneath the starlit canvas,
Nights wrapped in a silvery hue,
Whispers of winter fill the air,
As dreams of snowflakes come true.

Flames flicker in the hearth's embrace,
Casting warmth on faces aglow,
While the world beyond lies sleeping,
In blankets of shimmering snow.

Outside, the stillness is profound,
Each breath a whisper, soft and light,
In the arms of the midnight hour,
We cherish these twinkling winter nights.

Frosty patterns lace the windows,
Nature's artistry forged with grace,
As the universe holds its secrets,
In this magic, we find our place.

Dance with shadows of the flickering light,
Let the chill wrap you like a sheet,
For in the heart of winter's embrace,
A symphony of stars, we greet.

Radiant Chill

A radiant chill descends at dusk,
Starlight dances on the ice,
Every breath a cloud of wonder,
In this world, so cold and nice.

Blankets of snow hug the ground,
Softly muffling every sound,
While the moon's halo shines above,
In this winter dream, we're found.

Icicles hang like crystal dreams,
Nature's sculptures, bold and grand,
Painting stories in the twilight,
Just like magic, in our hands.

Through the branches, whispers travel,
Carrying secrets of the night,
As we bask in this cool splendor,
Wrapped in winter's pure delight.

So let the chill embrace your spirit,
For in the cold, we find our thrill,
A reminder of the beauty,
In this wondrous, radiant chill.

Drifting in Radiance

Softly glows the morning light,
As dreams begin to take their flight.
Whispers in the golden air,
Hopeful hearts begin to dare.

Dance of shadows on the ground,
In the silence, joy is found.
Colors merge in gentle sway,
Guiding souls along the way.

Every beam a story tells,
Where the light and spirit dwells.
Beneath the sky, wide and grand,
We will rise, hand in hand.

Catch the spark, embrace the day,
Let the worries drift away.
In the warmth, our spirits soar,
Together, we will seek for more.

Radiance in every glance,
In this moment, we will dance.
Through the clouds, we find our place,
Lost in love's eternal grace.

Sublime Snowlight

Whispers fall like feathers light,
Blankets draped in purest white.
Underneath the quiet glow,
Nature hushed, we move slow.

Crystal dreams on branches rest,
Every flake a gentle jest.
In this realm of serene night,
Hearts are warmed by snow's delight.

Silvery paths lead us near,
Footprints echo, crystal clear.
In the stillness, peace unfolds,
Stories written, yet untold.

Stars above in velvet sky,
Watch the world as we drift by.
Wrapped in winter's soft embrace,
Finding magic in this space.

Time stands still, our spirits blend,
In this moment, winter's friend.
Sublime whispers, dreams ignite,
Lost forever in snowlight.

Hope in the Frost

Morning breaks with icy breath,
Nature sleeping, still as death.
Yet beneath the frozen crust,
Lies the promise, hope and trust.

Silent trees with branches bare,
Hold the warmth of love and care.
In the frost, a spark will gleam,
Awakening each frozen dream.

Sunrise touches frosty ground,
Waking life all around.
In each glimmer, light returns,
As the flame of hope still burns.

Though the chill may pierce the skin,
We shall find the strength within.
Each breath taken, pure and free,
Hope reborn in you, in me.

Through the frost, we rise anew,
With each step, we feel the hue.
In the cold, our hearts ignite,
Guided by the morning light.

Resplendent Remnants

Echoes of what used to be,
Whispers soft, a memory.
Fragments held in tender grace,
Resplendent remnants of this place.

Colors fade but do not die,
In our hearts, they linger nigh.
Lessons learned and moments shared,
In the silence, souls have bared.

Through the trials, joy still sings,
In the pain, the beauty clings.
Every scar tells of our fight,
Resplendent remnants, purest light.

Time may change the world we know,
Yet within, the spirit grows.
In the shadows, wisdom's found,
In the heart, we stand our ground.

Treasures buried, love's embrace,
In each memory, find your place.
Resplendent remnants, soft and true,
In every heart, they've shaped anew.

Frosted Reverie

In a land where silence reigns,
Snowflakes dance on winter's breath,
Whispers of the chilly plains,
A world wrapped in icy sheath.

Dreams are woven with the frost,
Each breath a cloud in the night,
Memories of warmth now lost,
Underneath the pale moonlight.

Footsteps crunch on glistening ground,
Echoes of laughter in the cold,
Nature's beauty all around,
In this tapestry of gold.

Trees adorned with diamonds bright,
Branches heavy with the snow,
Glistening under stars so white,
Such a wondrous, peaceful show.

When the morning light appears,
Casting rays on frozen streams,
I embrace the planet's tears,
In this frosted realm of dreams.

Winter's Diamond Veil

A blanket soft, of pristine white,
Covers earth in gentle grace,
Nature's touch, a pure delight,
In this cold and sacred space.

Underneath the twilight's gleam,
Stars like diamonds from above,
Whispers of a dreamy theme,
Wrap the world in frozen love.

Footsteps lead through snow-kissed paths,
Crickets fade to stillness clear,
Here the air with magic laughs,
Winter's song, for all to hear.

Each flake falls with quiet ease,
Carving wonders, soft and bright,
Frozen trees swaying with the breeze,
Veils of mist in morning light.

In the heart of winter's chill,
I find warmth, I find my way,
With the promise, soft and still,
Of the spring that comes to play.

Delicate Spectacle

Gentle flakes in swirling flight,
Frosty whispers through the air,
Nature shows her purest light,
Beauty found in coldest care.

Snowmen rise with cheerful smiles,
Children laugh, their joy abounds,
Winter dreams span countless miles,
In this realm where magic sounds.

Mittens warm hands, cheeks aglow,
Snowflakes melt on eager tongues,
Every moment starts to flow,
With the songs of winter's songs.

Icicles hang like crystal tears,
Dripping in the morning sun,
Wonders born in frosty years,
A delicate dance begun.

In this canvas painted white,
Nature's brush strokes wide and free,
Delicate moments take flight,
In perfect winter reverie.

Chilly Radiance

The world adorned in icy glow,
Every corner sparkles bright,
A chilly breath, the winds do blow,
Underneath the starry light.

Frosty trees in frosted lace,
Whispers below the moonlit sky,
Nature's art, a pure embrace,
Where all worries drift and fly.

In the silence, hearts aligned,
Peaceful moments, still and true,
In the chill, new warmth we find,
With each step, the world anew.

Frozen lakes, a flawless sheet,
Reflecting dreams of what might be,
In this winter, bittersweet,
A dance of nature's mastery.

When the sun begins to rise,
Colors burst in broad arcs wide,
Chilly radiance fills the skies,
In this beauty, I confide.

Pervasive Frostbite

Chill winds whisper through the trees,
Fingers numb against the freeze.
A hush of snow blankets the ground,
In this quiet, no warmth is found.

Icicles hang like daggers near,
Nature's breath brings thoughts of fear.
Each step crunches on the white,
Lost in shadows, fading light.

Hearts grow heavy with the cold,
Stories of warmth, quietly told.
Underneath the frozen crust,
Lies a world that waits for us.

Eyes like stars in a blackened night,
Glimmer softly, holding tight.
Through the frost, a spark will rise,
Awakening life beneath the skies.

When spring's arrival clears the air,
We will bask in sunlight's glare.
Yet in memories, frostbite lingers,
Whispered tales through time's cold fingers.

Polished Icescapes

A world of glass beneath my feet,
Where dreams and reality meet.
Glistening surfaces catch the glow,
Of twinkling stars all covered in snow.

Mountains dressed in crystal white,
Reflecting warmth of the pale moonlight.
Every flake a unique work of art,
Whispers of winter that tug at the heart.

Frozen rivers gently flow,
In their stillness, secrets glow.
Echoes of laughter fill the air,
As skaters dance without a care.

Glistening branches brush the sky,
While frosty breezes silently sigh.
In this icy realm, time stands still,
Filling each moment with quiet thrill.

As dawn breaks with softest hue,
The polished beauty comes into view.
Nature's canvas, a wondrous sight,
In the embrace of winter's night.

Reflections of Winter

In windows, the world is a frosty frame,
Captured wonders, never the same.
Reflecting light with a gentle grace,
A moment held in winter's embrace.

Footprints trace a story untold,
Wandering through the chill so bold.
Each breath a cloud, a fleeting sign,
Of warmth concealed in hearts divine.

Beneath the frost, life's pulse remains,
Whispers echo through winding lanes.
Tales of warmth, though hidden so deep,
In silence, nature finds her sleep.

The sun sinks low, a golden gleam,
Painting shadows in twilight's dream.
A quiet hush blankets the night,
As stars awaken to share their light.

Yet in the echoes of frozen air,
Hope emerges with tender care.
For every end that winter brings,
Is a promise of rebirth in spring's wings.

Shimmering Nostalgia

Memories dance like snowflakes swirl,
In the soft glow of a frozen world.
A time once sweet, now tinged with frost,
In shimmering moments, we find what's lost.

Laughter rings through the chilly air,
Reminders linger, we still care.
Each icy breath holds a story dear,
Of warmth and love, the heart can steer.

Fires crackle with a gentle light,
As shadows swirl in the quiet night.
Cocoa warms our hands like dreams,
While outside, the wind softly screams.

Paths we wandered, side by side,
Now marked by snow, memories abide.
In the stillness, we hold them tight,
Wrapped in the magic of winter's night.

So here we stand, as seasons change,
In nostalgia's grip, we feel the strange.
For in each flake that falls anew,
Lies a heartbeat, a memory of you.

Icy Starfall

In the night, stars are falling,
Whispers of ice softly calling.
Beneath the chill of twilight's breath,
Dreams of winter, dance with death.

Timid glimmers touch the ground,
Covering silence with a sound.
Glints of silver, a cosmic show,
Cold and bright, they swiftly flow.

Frosty air begins to freeze,
Echoes of night hum through the trees.
Glittering paths where shadows blend,
Icy starfall, time won't mend.

Above, a canopy of sparkles gleam,
Soft and silent, like a dream.
Sparkles fade at dawn's first light,
Whispers lost to morning bright.

In the heart where wonder's woven,
Memories linger, unspoken.
Underneath the tapestry wide,
Icy starfall, a magic guide.

Frosted Moonbeams

Softly sighing through the night,
Frosted moonbeams, pure and bright.
Kissing hills with tender grace,
Illuminating nature's face.

In the silence, shadows play,
Moonlit whispers, gently sway.
Each beam a thread, silvered, fine,
Crafting dreams in frosted line.

Stars above, a distant choir,
Guiding hearts through night's desire.
Underneath a velvet sky,
Frosted glimmers drifting by.

Nature's canvas, pure delight,
Adorned in crystals, soft and light.
Every moment, tranquil streams,
Lost in soft and frosted dreams.

When dawn approaches, shadows release,
Moonbeams fade, finding peace.
Yet, in memory they'll remain,
Frosted whispers, sweet refrain.

Luminous Frost

Morning breaks with whispered light,
Luminous frost, a dazzling sight.
Crystals dance on blades of grass,
Glimmers held as moments pass.

Chill embraces every face,
Nature wrapped in winter's lace.
Frosted branches gently sway,
In the golden hues of day.

Each sparkle tells a silent tale,
Of chilly nights and night's exhale.
With warmth of sun, they slowly fade,
Memories of the night's parade.

In this wonder, joy is found,
Frozen beauty all around.
Luminous frost, a fleeting sign,
Crafted visions, pure, divine.

As evening falls, the cycle spins,
Frost returns as daylight thins.
In the heart, a spark remains,
Luminous frost, nature's chains.

Gleaming Tundra

In the stillness, beauty gleams,
Gleaming tundra, frozen dreams.
Across the vast and white expanse,
Nature's wonders, in a trance.

Beneath the sky, a crystal layer,
Winds weave stories, soft and rare.
Whispers float on frosty air,
In this silence, magic's fair.

Echoes of the past arise,
Where land meets the endless skies.
Footprints left in purest snow,
Gleaming tundra, where dreams flow.

In the twilight, shadows stretch,
Magic weaves, our hearts to fetch.
With every glint, a promise made,
A bond of nature, never fade.

As dawn unfolds, the chill remains,
Gleaming tundra, love's refrains.
In this beauty, souls align,
Underneath the frost's design.

Celestial Chill

Stars twinkle in the night,
A blanket of frost takes flight.
Whispers of the cosmic air,
Moonbeams dance without a care.

Silent spires of silver light,
Guide the wandering souls in flight.
Each breath a cloud of frosty glow,
In the stillness, time moves slow.

Frozen whispers touch the ground,
In the hush, peace can be found.
The cosmos speaks in gentle tones,
In the cold, we find our homes.

Crystals fall from heaven's hand,
Painting patterns on the land.
Each flake tells a story bright,
Of a world wrapped in the night.

Underneath the vast expanse,
We stand in awe, caught in a trance.
Celestial wonders ever near,
In the chill, there's naught to fear.

Sapphire Skies

Endless blue, a sea above,
Where birds take wing, and dreams do shove.
The sunbeams play on fields of gold,
Whispers of warm, a tale retold.

Clouds like cotton softly drift,
In sapphire skies, our spirits lift.
A canvas broad, a painter's delight,
Embracing day, embracing night.

Winds caress the tranquil ground,
In this beauty, solace found.
Moments linger, time stands still,
In sapphire skies, the heart can fill.

As twilight falls, a gentle hue,
The sky ignites, a million blue.
Stars emerge from the deep abyss,
In the calm, we find our bliss.

Underneath this painted dome,
We find the peace that feels like home.
Sapphire skies, a love profound,
In their embrace, we are unbound.

Moonlit Glimmer

Silver beams on tranquil seas,
Whispers of the night do tease.
Ripples shimmer in soft light,
Moonlit glimmers shine so bright.

Softly serenade the trees,
In the night, a gentle breeze.
Dancing shadows sway and play,
While the moon keeps dark at bay.

Stars aligned in a velvet spread,
Wish upon them, dreams are fed.
Every spark, a tale to tell,
In this night, all seems well.

Glistening paths on rivers flow,
With each wave, new stories grow.
Moonlit glimmer, a soft embrace,
In this moment, find your place.

In the hush, the world feels right,
Under stars, hearts take flight.
Moonlit dreams, forever stay,
Guiding souls along their way.

Frosted Daggers

Sharp and cold, the winter's bite,
Frosted daggers glint in light.
Nature's art, so fierce and bright,
In the chill, a fierce delight.

Icicles hang like silver fangs,
Winter's grip through landscape clangs.
Every branch adorned with care,
Frosty patterns everywhere.

In the morning's crisp embrace,
Each breath condenses in this space.
The world a canvas pure and white,
Frosted daggers cut the night.

Silent forests, still and bare,
Whispers float upon the air.
A fragile beauty, sharp yet sweet,
In the cold, our hearts compete.

As sunlight breaks the frozen gloom,
A warm glow chases off the doom.
Still, the daggers hold their charm,
In winter's grasp, we find our calm.

Frosted Dreams

In the hush of the night, soft and bright,
A blanket of white, a frosty light.
Whispers of snowflakes dance through the air,
Dreams wrapped in winter, beyond compare.

Silent shadows creep, under the moon,
Curling up close, in a silver tune.
Each breath a cloud, in the chilly breeze,
Frosted dreams linger, like gentle freeze.

Footprints in snow, a story untold,
Secrets of winter, through silence unfold.
The sparkle of stars, in a vast night sky,
Illuminates the world, as time drifts by.

Among the stillness, hope takes its flight,
In frosted dreams, everything feels right.
Wrapped in the magic, that winter bestows,
Hearts beat with joy, as the cold wind blows.

Together we wander, hand in hand tight,
Facing the chill, hearts brave and light.
In the realm of dreams, where the snowflakes fall,
Frosted visions unite us all.

Crystal Whispers

Beneath the branches, where shadows play,
Crystal whispers beckon, in the light of day.
Glimmers of magic, in the dew's embrace,
Nature's soft secrets, in this tranquil space.

Every shimmering breath, a soft serenade,
Tickling the senses, as colors invade.
Wind carries stories, through leaves that sway,
Found in the silence, like dreams on display.

Ripples of laughter, through the bubbling brook,
Echoes of joy in every nook.
Fleeting moments caught, in crystalline grace,
Kissed by the sun in this enchanted place.

With each gentle breeze, the world comes alive,
In crystal whispers, our spirits thrive.
Harmony dances, in the glint of the light,
All around us, everything feels right.

With hearts wide open, we wander and roam,
In the land of enchantment, we've found our home.
Crystal whispers guide us, through the shimmering trees,
In this sacred space, we are forever free.

Shimmering Silence

In the quiet dusk, where shadows blend,
Shimmering silence, a soothing friend.
Stars peek through clouds, a twinkling show,
Whispers of twilight, in the soft glow.

Moonlight caresses the world so mild,
Embracing the night, like a dreaming child.
Each flicker of light reveals hidden charms,
Wrapped in the night, safe in its arms.

Gentle waves lap at the shore's embrace,
In shimmering silence, we find our place.
Moments like fireflies, caught in the air,
Flashes of peace, show love's gentle care.

With every heartbeat, a rhythm so clear,
Echoes of stillness, love draws near.
In the realm of dreams, where the quiet reigns,
Shimmering silence, the heart sustains.

So let us linger, till night meets the dawn,
In the sparkling stillness, we are reborn.
For within the silence, we find our way,
Guided by stars, till the break of day.

Icy Radiance

In the chill of dawn, a world aglow,
Icy radiance dances on winter's bow.
Crystals refract through the morning light,
Each breath a whisper, as day turns bright.

Snowflakes twirl softly, like hushed ballet,
Artistry painted in white and gray.
Nature adorned in her finest array,
A frosty embrace at the start of the day.

Frosted branches stretch, seeking the sun,
In icy radiance, the day has begun.
With every sparkle, joy takes its flight,
Awakening dreams in the morning light.

The world is at peace, wrapped in the chill,
Moments like jewels, hearts warm and still.
In this gentle glow, we find our chance,
To dance through the wonder, lost in romance.

So let us embrace, this season of ice,
Where beauty prevails, and dreams entice.
With icy radiance, our spirits rise high,
In this wondrous realm, we forever lie.

Luster of the Abyss

In deep and dark, where shadows play,
The whispers of the night convey.
A dance of light, a fleeting gleam,
The silence wraps us in a dream.

Among the waves, the secrets dwell,
In depths where silence weaves its spell.
A glimmer here, a shimmer there,
The luster shines, beyond compare.

The pull of tides, the urge to dive,
In abysm deep, the depths alive.
With every stroke, a spark ignites,
In blackened homes, in hidden sights.

The treasure sought beneath the brine,
In every breath, the depths entwine.
A siren's call, the heart obeys,
In murky dark, a world ablaze.

So come and swim, embrace the night,
In luster's grasp, the soul takes flight.
For in the abyss, where few have trod,
A realm of dreams, beneath the sod.

Silent Dazzle

Beneath the moon's soft silver glow,
A gentle hush, where breezes flow.
The stars above begin to twirl,
In quiet dazzle, night unfurls.

A stillness wraps the world anew,
In whispered tones, the dreams ensue.
The heartbeats mark the passing time,
In silent rhythm, pure as rhyme.

Each twinkle sparks a fleeting thought,
In tranquil moments, peace is caught.
The night reveals its shimmering face,
In secret spaces, tender grace.

Endless wonder fills the air,
In every glance, a soft affair.
A constellation, bright and rare,
In silence, love is laid bare.

So linger long beneath the skies,
In silent dazzle, time defies.
With every breath, the night sings clear,
In hushed delight, we hold it dear.

Shimmer on the Surface

The lake reflects the morning light,
With glimmers bright, a pure delight.
Each ripple dances, soft and free,
A sparkling veil, tranquility.

The gentle breeze caresses skin,
As nature stirs, the day begins.
A symphony of hues ignite,
The shimmer whispers, calm and bright.

Among the reeds, small creatures play,
In playful arcs, they seize the day.
With every splash, a joy unfolds,
The surface glistens, stories told.

A fleeting glimpse, a moment caught,
In shimmering waves, dreams are sought.
The world awakes, each breath anew,
In nature's mirror, life breaks through.

So take a step toward the shore,
And feel the peace that's here in store.
In shimmer's dance, let spirit soar,
On surface lanes, forevermore.

Serene Glimmers

At dawn's embrace, the world ignites,
With pastel strokes and soft delights.
A canvas fresh, a silent cheer,
In every glimmer, dreams appear.

The mountains rise, majestic, still,
As morning wraps the vale at will.
With every breath, the hearts collide,
In serene glimmers, love resides.

The rivers sing their lulling song,
In gentle tones, where we belong.
A tranquil space, where worries cease,
In nature's arms, we find our peace.

Beneath the trees, the shadows dance,
In dappled light, a fleeting chance.
To pause and feel the moments breathe,
In glimmers soft, we take our leave.

So close your eyes, and let it flow,
In serene glimmers, let love grow.
For life's a gift, a fleeting spark,
In every heart, ignites the dark.

Frosted Lullabies

Whispers glide on winter's breath,
Moonlight drapes the world in rest.
Snowflakes dance like dreams untold,
A quiet hush, a magic hold.

Sleepy trees wear coats of white,
Stars adorn the velvet night.
Every flake, a song of cheer,
Cradling hearts, dispelling fear.

With each chill, a soft embrace,
Nature's warmth in frozen space.
Awake the dreams that softly flow,
In slumber's arms, we gently glow.

Footsteps fade on frosted ground,
Where peaceful thoughts are softly found.
In this world of ice and light,
Lullabies weave through the night.

Hold this moment, pure and bright,
Frosted magic, pure delight.
With every breath, let worries cease,
Winter's touch brings lasting peace.

Frigid Brilliance

In the stillness, cold so bright,
Crystals gleam in morning light.
Every branch in silver dressed,
Nature's jewel, truly blessed.

Snowdrifts swirl like diamonds rare,
Whisper secrets in the air.
An icy canvas stretched wide,
Frigid brilliance, beauty's pride.

Frost-kissed whispers, soft embrace,
Time stands still in this vast space.
A fleeting glance of nature's art,
Frigid brilliance warms the heart.

Beneath the frost, life's pulse remains,
Hidden joys in winter's reins.
In the quiet, hopes take flight,
Shining softly through the night.

Let the chill embrace our dreams,
In the dark, a glowing gleam.
Frigid brilliance guides the way,
Through this night, into the day.

Light Within the Ice

The world, a canvas wrapped in frost,
Beauty found in what is lost.
In icy veins, a pulse of gold,
A flicker of warmth, story told.

Glistening shards, where sunlight breaks,
Illuminate the path we take.
Hidden treasures, cold and clear,
Light within the ice draws near.

Each frozen breath, a moment seized,
Nature whispers, all are pleased.
In shadows deep, a brightening sigh,
The heart's warmth cannot die.

Warming embers beneath the chill,
Fires of hope that gently thrill.
Beneath the frost, bright spirits rise,
Carried forth on winter's sighs.

With every step, we forge the night,
Finding love in cold's embrace tight.
Through icy paths, we walk as one,
In the light, the journey's begun.

Bewitched by Winter

Woven tales in snowbound nights,
Magic brims with frosty sights.
Each corner holds a story dear,
Bewitched by winter, losing fear.

Frosty breath and starlit skies,
Whispers dance as silence flies.
In every flake, a wish ignites,
Transforming dreams on frosty nights.

Beneath the moon's enchanted glow,
Wonders bloom in icy flow.
In the stillness, hearts align,
As winter paints with love divine.

Bewitched by nature's gentle grace,
We find our truth in frozen space.
Every chill, a lover's sigh,
Wrapped in warmth, we wander high.

In this magic, we become,
A symphony of winter's hum.
Together in this season's thrall,
Bewitched by winter, we embrace all.

Secrets Beneath the Chill

In whispers soft, the cold confides,
Stories lost where silence hides.
Beneath the frost, the secrets sleep,
Guarded dreams in layers deep.

Trees adorned in icy lace,
Nature's breath, a frozen grace.
Footsteps echo on the ground,
In the hush, the truth is found.

Crystal shards in morning light,
Glimmering jewels, pure and bright.
Time stands still in this retreat,
Where heartbeats and the cold can meet.

Shadows dance upon the snow,
As the chill begins to grow.
Veils of white cloak all around,
Whispers of the lost abound.

Secrets shimmer, caught in air,
Frigid tales that nature shares.
The winter holds a mystic charm,
Within its grasp, we find our calm.

Glimpses of Frosted Dawn

A soft glow breaks the dark of night,
Where frost encases all in white.
Glistening woods in gentle cheer,
Whispering news winter is here.

The sun peeks through with tender grace,
Kissing earth in a warm embrace.
Every branch and every leaf,
Cloaked in magic, free from grief.

Colors bloom where frost has fled,
A world revived, where dreams are fed.
Light dances on the quilted snow,
Artistry in the morning's glow.

Echoes of the chill persist,
Yet warmth escapes through winter's mist.
Moments linger, softly sway,
As dawn reveals the brightening day.

In every breath, the chill remains,
Infusing life with crystal chains.
Hope emerges in frigid air,
Glimpses of dawn, so rare and fair.

Frigid Zen

Among the pines, a stillness grows,
In every flake, tranquility flows.
Breath of winter, sharp and clear,
Invites the heart to draw near.

Snowflakes fall like whispered thoughts,
Blanketing the world it caught.
In stillness deep, a calm prevails,
The silence weaves its sacred trails.

Each step crunches in the snow,
A moment's pause, time's gentle flow.
Frigid air, a lucid balm,
In frozen peace, we find our calm.

Embrace the chill, let worries flee,
The winter's gift of clarity.
Mind unwinds in crystal breath,
Finding life within the death.

Where shadows stretch and daylight dims,
Solitude's song in nature swims.
Frigid Zen, a simple grace,
Within the cold, we find our place.

Blinding Winter Gleam

A blinding burst of white and light,
Dancing sparkles through the night.
Winter's breath upon the ground,
Magic woven all around.

The world transformed in purest hue,
Every flake, a diamond's view.
Radiance breaks the darkest gloom,
In winter's heart, the flowers bloom.

Mountains high with snowy crowns,
Glinting gold in sunset towns.
Rivers freeze, a tranquil sheen,
A landscape vast, crisp and serene.

Every glimmer tells a tale,
Of freezing winds and lonesome trails.
Stillness reigns, the beauty steams,
Life ignites in winter's dreams.

In this gleam, our spirits rise,
Chasing sunsets, painted skies.
Bound by cold, yet so alive,
Through blinding frost, we learn to thrive.

Polished Snowscape

A blanket of white, so pure and deep,
Whispers of winter, where silence sleeps.
Footprints fade softly, lost in the drift,
Nature's canvas, a magical gift.

Trees cloaked in frost, like silver lace,
Breathe in the chill, feel time slow its pace.
Dreams in the snowflakes, soft as a sigh,
In this serene world, let your worries fly.

Mountains stand guard, timeless and grand,
Echoes of stillness across the land.
Sunlight breaks through, a gentle embrace,
In polished snowscape, we find our grace.

Crisp air awakens the soul from rest,
Wrapped in a stillness, we feel so blessed.
Each flake a story, unique and bright,
In the heart of winter, everything feels right.

Night descends softly, the stars ignite,
Under the moon, everything feels light.
The world now sparkles, a tranquil glow,
In polished snowscape, peace starts to flow.

Celestial Glimmers

Stars sprinkle the night, twinkling so high,
Painting the heavens, a cosmic sigh.
Whispers of light dance through the blue,
In celestial glimmers, dreams feel anew.

The moon's silver face watches us near,
Illuminating paths, dispelling our fear.
Galaxies swirl in a timeless embrace,
In this vast universe, we find our place.

Nebulas blossom, colors collide,
Infinite wonders, our hearts open wide.
Each sparkling light, a story untold,
In celestial glimmers, mysteries unfold.

Comets may blaze across skies so deep,
Moments a'whirl that we long to keep.
With every glance, our spirits ignite,
In this endless cosmos, we find our light.

Dusk gently fades, the night takes its throne,
Embracing each dream that we've ever known.
In celestial glimmers, we hold our fate,
Woven with starlight, beautifully great.

Sparkling Icicles

Hanging like crystals, so sharp and bright,
Captured reflections in the soft sunlight.
Nature's daggers, suspended in time,
Sparkling icicles, a chilling rhyme.

Water's embrace forms each delicate thread,
Whispers of winter, where beauty is bred.
A frozen artistry, pure and refined,
In these sharp wonders, warmth we must find.

Drip-drip they fall, like laughter in air,
Melodies echo, a song everywhere.
Each drop a promise, a fleeting chance,
In sparkling icicles, the seasons dance.

Winter's breath hangs, a silvery trail,
Crafting the scenes where the heart will sail.
Frozen moments, a dreamer's delight,
Sparkling icicles in the soft twilight.

The sun bids farewell, in colors it plays,
Soft magentas and golds sing sweet arrays.
Under their shimmer, we rest for a while,
In sparkling icicles, we find our smile.

Glistening Twilight

When day starts to fade, the sky turns to gold,
Whispers of magic in shadows unfold.
Crimson and violet paint the horizon,
In glistening twilight, our hopes will rise on.

The soft breeze carries a lullaby's tune,
Crickets awaken beneath the bright moon.
The stars slowly twinkle, a silent delight,
In glistening twilight, the world feels just right.

Each breath is a treasure, a moment to keep,
As colors unite, the earth starts to sleep.
Dreams take their flight on the wings of the night,
In glistening twilight, we find pure insight.

Time seems to linger, wrapped in its hue,
Painting the canvas with magic anew.
A dance of the shadows, a sweet serenade,
In the quiet embrace, our worries evade.

So let the night gather, softly and bold,
As whispers of twilight its stories unfold.
In every heartbeat, a promise we write,
In glistening twilight, we bask in the light.

Shiny Fragments

Scattered gems on the ground,
Glimmers of light all around.
Whispers of stories untold,
In each fragment, dreams unfold.

Colors dance in the sun,
Reflecting joy, everyone.
A mosaic of moments bright,
Crafting a canvas of light.

In the breeze, they gently sway,
Telling secrets of the day.
A tapestry of the past,
Memories woven, forever to last.

Every shard holds a tale,
In silence, they softly unveil.
A treasure trove of the heart,
Each shiny piece a work of art.

Gathered close, they shine anew,
A beautiful dance in the dew.
In the twilight, they remain,
Forever etched in our brain.

Glistening Twilight

As day fades into night,
Stars begin to take flight.
The horizon blushes low,
A gentle, warm afterglow.

Whispers of the coming night,
The world wrapped in soft light.
Branches sway in evening's breeze,
Rustling softly like the trees.

Moonlight spills like silver streams,
Illuminating twilight dreams.
A tapestry of shadow and hue,
Painting the world, calm and true.

Each glimmer holds a sweet sigh,
Beneath the vast, open sky.
Time slows in this lovely place,
Where each moment finds its grace.

Crickets sing their lullabies,
Underneath the velvet skies.
In this peaceful, quiet night,
Hearts embrace the gentle light.

Dreamscape in Winter

Snowflakes drift, a soft ballet,
Covering the world in white array.
A silent hush, then laughter's song,
In this wonderland, we belong.

Footprints mark where we have been,
In crisp, cold air, our faces grin.
Childlike joy fills every heart,
As winter's magic takes its part.

The sky, a canvas of gray and blue,
Icy breath as dreams come true.
Hot cocoa warms our tiny hands,
By fireside, love understands.

In the woods, a hidden wight,
Glows beneath the pale moonlight.
Frosted whispers of the night,
Bring enchantment to our sight.

As shadows deepen, stars appear,
Shimmering bright, drawing near.
In this dreamscape, pure and bright,
We find peace in the winter's night.

Frosted Embers

In the hearth, the embers glow,
Frosted outside, soft and slow.
A warmth that dances, flickers right,
Casting shadows in the night.

Firelight sparkles on the wall,
As winter's chill begins to call.
Whispers echo through the trees,
Carried gently by the breeze.

Each spark, a memory held near,
Of laughter shared with those most dear.
In frozen stillness, hearts ignite,
Frosted embers shining bright.

Through the windows, snowflakes drift,
Nature's way, a precious gift.
With every glimmer, dreams arise,
In this warmth, true love never dies.

As night wraps close, stars take flight,
Frosted embers burn so bright.
In the silence, spirits dwell,
In warmth and love, all is well.

Frost-adorned Dreams

In the hush of winter's breath,
White blankets weave a soft caress,
Shimmering like silent wishes,
That dance in cold's sweet tenderness.

Each crystal holds a hidden tale,
Of magic spun in moonlit grace,
Footprints crunch in the quiet pale,
As dreams flutter through this frozen space.

Whispers of the past collide,
With moments caught in fragile light,
The earth adorned in frosty pride,
A canvas painted day and night.

Hearts are warmed by cozy fires,
Stories shared with gentle sighs,
As winter's charm softly inspires,
The dreams that lace the cold, vast skies.

Yet as dawn breaks, light will beam,
Melting layers of icy lace,
Leaving but a fleeting gleam,
Of frost-adorned dreams we embrace.

The Beauty of Stillness

In moments caught between the ticks,
The world holds breath, time gently sleeps,
A quiet charm in the music's mix,
Where beauty in stillness softly creeps.

Leaves whisper secrets to the ground,
As shadows blend with fading light,
In this space, a peace is found,
Where worries ebb and hearts take flight.

Sky painted in dusk's warm hues,
Reflects a calm on the lake's face,
With every ripple, the heart renews,
In nature's soothing, sweet embrace.

Birds perch still on swaying limbs,
As day bows down to night's cool reign,
The beauty of silence softly swims,
Through every fiber, erasing pain.

Embrace the pause, let spirits rise,
In this gentle lull, we find our way,
For in stillness, we realize,
Life's beauty shines in moments gray.

Tinsel-like Essence

Threads of gold in twinkling light,
Adorn our hearts this winter night,
Sparkling bright, they pull us near,
A tinsel-like essence, pure and clear.

Laughter dances on the breeze,
As memories weave through our minds,
In this moment, joy will tease,
Uniting souls, love intertwines.

Candles flicker with gentle grace,
Reflecting warmth in every face,
A tapestry of love and dreams,
Glistening softly, or so it seems.

With every cheer, the world ignites,
In shimmering colors, pulses gleam,
The night unfolds with pure delights,
Wrapping us in a glowing dream.

So let us toast to moments bright,
With tinsel-like essence filling the air,
For in these shards of gleaming light,
Life's sweetest treasures we will share.

Glinting Evenings

The sun surrenders to the night,
As stars emerge with twinkling sight,
Glinting softly like whispers rare,
Painting secrets in the air.

Gentle breezes brush the trees,
Swaying softly, dressed in ease,
In twilight's grasp, the world feels free,
As time unfurls its mystery.

Colors blend in a soft embrace,
Golden hues in a fading race,
Night's embrace begins to call,
Where shadows dance and echoes fall.

Under skies adorned with dreams,
The universe in stillness gleams,
While crickets sing a lullaby,
Echoing far beneath the sky.

So let us linger in this peace,
As glinting evenings gently tease,
Each moment savored, held so dear,
In whispered wishes, love draws near.

The Brightness of Winter

Snowflakes dance in icy air,
Crystals twinkle everywhere.
The world wrapped in a blanket white,
A stillness graces the winter night.

Frosted branches shine like glass,
Moments caught that lightly pass.
Whispers of a season's cheer,
Echoes softly, drawing near.

Children laugh in snowy bliss,
Frozen smiles, a fleeting kiss.
Sleds carve paths through fields of white,
Joyful shouts in pure delight.

The moon hangs low in azure skies,
Casting shadows, wise and shy.
In this peaceful, frozen nest,
Winter holds its quiet rest.

As twilight falls, the stars appear,
Each a spark that brings us near.
The brightness of this winter day,
Sings of beauty, come what may.

Ethereal Echoes

Whispers travel on the breeze,
Floating softly through the trees.
Voices dance in twilight's glow,
Secrets shared, we come to know.

In the stillness, time stands still,
Echoes linger, soft and shrill.
Fleeting moments, dreams in flight,
Carving pathways through the night.

Starlit skies above our heads,
Painted hues in indigo spreads.
Ethereal songs from far away,
Guide our hearts where shadows play.

A gentle touch upon our skin,
An invitation to begin.
In this realm where spirits weave,
We find ourselves, we dare to believe.

Each sound a memory's embrace,
Calling forth a timeless space.
Together lost in night's expanse,
We surrender to the dance.

Diamonds on the Snow

Winter's charm in glistening light,
Diamonds shimmering, pure and bright.
Each flake unique, a work of art,
Nature's jewels, that warm the heart.

Underneath the pale moon's beam,
Snowflakes swirl like a waking dream.
Footsteps crunch in the silvered night,
Dancing shadows, fleeting sight.

Frosty breath in the chilly air,
Bitter winds whisper, soft and rare.
A canvas spread, so wide, so deep,
Inviting us to laugh, to leap.

Warm fires crackle, flickering glow,
Illuminating diamonds on the snow.
With every breath, we find our place,
In winter's calm, a warm embrace.

As day breaks bright on winter's face,
These diamonds dwell in nature's grace.
A fleeting beauty, a moment's cheer,
In the heart's treasure, always near.

Transient Glimmers

In golden dawn, the world awakes,
A dance of light that softly shakes.
Transient glimmers grace the morn,
Each ray of sun, a dream reborn.

Dew drops cling to blades of grass,
Nature's jewels as moments pass.
Shadows play across the ground,
In whispered tales, our joy is found.

Time slips by like grains of sand,
Each fleeting glance, a gentle hand.
Eager hearts chase after time,
Finding music in each rhyme.

Evening clouds in splendid hues,
Render skies in prism views.
As twilight whispers, day bids adieu,
The heart remembers what it knew.

In these glimmers, memories stay,
Bright reminders of yesterday.
We hold each transient moment dear,
In every sigh, they linger near.

Aurora's Kiss

In the night sky dances bright,
A curtain of colors, pure delight.
Whispers of magic in the air,
Nature's beauty, beyond compare.

With each wave, the heavens sigh,
As stars twinkle, a lullaby.
The world below, in silence, waits,
For the dawn that softly greets.

Colors blend in a soft embrace,
Streaks of pink and green interlace.
A fleeting moment, still and true,
Wrapped in wonder, just me and you.

The night fades, but memories stay,
Of Aurora's kiss, a bright display.
In dreams we'll chase that radiant glow,
Together beneath the skies aglow.

So let us wander, hand in hand,
Through fields of starlight, across the land.
In every shimmer, in every beam,
We'll find the magic in our dream.

Icicle Serenade

With every drip, a note rings clear,
An icicle sings, a tune so dear.
Winter's breath in graceful arcs,
Hangs like jewels, where beauty sparks.

Beneath the frost, a silence deep,
The world is still, all hushed in sleep.
Nature's rhythm, so soft, so sweet,
Plays a melody beneath our feet.

Sparkling crystals catch the light,
Glistening softly in the night.
A fragile song, a fleeting sound,
In this chilly realm, magic found.

As the sun warms the frozen land,
Icicles dance, a glowing band.
Their serenade fades, yet remains,
In winter's heart, where beauty gains.

So listen close, as shadows play,
To the icicles' serenade today.
In every droplet, in every chime,
Winter whispers, a tale sublime.

Dazzle of the Slopes

On snowy peaks, the sunlight beams,
A world transformed in winter dreams.
Skis carve paths through purest white,
With each turn, our spirits bright.

The laughter rings, a joyful sound,
As snowflakes swirl around the ground.
Riding high on winter's grace,
We find our bliss in this embrace.

In the crisp air, we glide and sway,
Dazzled by this winter's play.
Every moment, a leap of joy,
In this paradise, we feel like a boy.

Hot cocoa waits, a warming treat,
As we gather, tired but sweet.
Stories shared by the glowing fire,
In this magic, we never tire.

So let the snowflakes fall like dreams,
In the dazzling light, life redeems.
With every slide, each joyful shout,
The slopes whisper love, there's no doubt.

Shining Winter Veil

Underneath a blanket white,
The world is hidden, pure, and bright.
Trees wear coats of glimmering snow,
While silence wraps the earth below.

With every breath, a frosty kiss,
Winter's song, we cannot miss.
Each flake a dancer, swirling low,
In the quiet, magic grows.

Footprints crunch on frozen ground,
A joyful echo all around.
In this wonderland, hearts entwine,
As day fades softly, stars align.

The moonlight weaves its silver thread,
Across the fields where dreams are bred.
In the stillness, hope takes flight,
Wrapped in winter's softest light.

So cherish moments, pure and real,
Within this shining winter veil.
In every sparkle, in every sigh,
We find the magic, you and I.

Frosted Lullabies

Winter whispers softly, light and clear,
Crystals dancing gently, drawing near.
Dreams wrapped in white, a blanket of peace,
Under the stars, let all worries cease.

Icicles hang like jewels on the eaves,
Quietly embracing what the night weaves.
Each breath a mist, a melody's sigh,
In the embrace of frost, we learn to fly.

Moonlight waltzes over fields of snow,
Guiding lost souls with its radiant glow.
Through the silence, the heartbeats align,
In the frosted magic, we intertwine.

Softly the night cradles dreams anew,
In the hush of the world, hope's gentle hue.
Pulled from the shadows, the laughter takes flight,
Wrapped in the warmth of a winter's night.

Frozen in time, the moments we share,
Echoing softly like whispers of prayer.
Here in this stillness, in love we find grace,
Frosted lullabies, our sacred space.

Luminous Chill

A frosty shimmer on the window pane,
Whispers of magic, a sweet refrain.
In the night's embrace, all shadows are bright,
Flickering softly in luminous light.

Stars glance down like diamonds in the deep,
Guardians of secrets that silence will keep.
With every breath, the world seems to freeze,
Wrapped in the wonder of winter's sweet tease.

A hush falls heavy, a blanket of calm,
Gentle reminders of nature's soft balm.
Each flake that descends, a story untold,
Glistening softly in the night's hold.

As hearts beat in time with the ticking clock,
Silence woven deep within every block.
Under the moon, the chill feels alive,
In luminous dreams, our spirits will thrive.

Frosted branches sway with the night's soft sigh,
Winter's sweet grace as the moments pass by.
Huddled together, under blankets of night,
In the luminous chill, our souls feel the light.

Sparkle of the Night

Under the blanket of a velvet sky,
Stars wink brightly, like diamonds on high.
Each twinkle a whisper, a secret shared,
In the sparkle of night, souls are ensnared.

Moonlight cascades through the branches bare,
Painting the world with a silvery flare.
Dancing on pathways where shadows converge,
In the quiet of night, our spirits emerge.

Cold winds embrace the shimmering scene,
Nature's artwork, serene and pristine.
With every heartbeat, the magic unfolds,
In the sparkle of night, our dreams take hold.

Frost-kissed horizons invite us to roam,
Guiding our steps as we wander home.
With laughter and love, we make our own light,
Finding our way in the sparkle of night.

In the embrace of the stars' gentle glow,
Hope's tender murmur sets our spirits aglow.
As we close our eyes, with hearts open wide,
In the sparkle of night, we find our guide.

Moonlit Ice

Reflections shimmer on the frozen lake,
Under the moon where the wild things wake.
Silvery pathways unfold in the dark,
Guided by starlight, each step leaves a mark.

The world holds its breath, a moment so rare,
Nature's soft canvas, suspended in air.
Crickets whisper secrets to the night,
In moonlit ice, everything feels right.

A dance of shadows on the surface vast,
Echoes of laughter from memories past.
As the night deepens, our spirits ignite,
In the silvery glow of the moonlit night.

Time melts away, like snow on the ground,
In the beauty of stillness, peace can be found.
With hearts intertwined, we embrace the freeze,
On moonlit ice, sweet serenity glees.

As dawn breaks softly, casting gold on white,
We hold this moment, a treasure, so bright.
In the depth of our dreams, forever we'll stay,
In the warmth of the sun, chasing shadows away.

Subtle Radiance

In twilight's soft embrace we find,
A glow that dances, warm yet kind.
Whispers of light through branches weave,
A gentle touch that makes us believe.

Moonlit secrets softly told,
Mysterious hues in silver and gold.
Each flicker tells a tale anew,
Of dreams unspoken, yet shining through.

The stars begin to softly gleam,
Bathing the world in a tender beam.
Hearts alight with pure delight,
Guided by the subtle light.

Shadows retreat as the night draws nigh,
Under the vast, eternal sky.
A shimmer lingers, faint but clear,
In every moment, love draws near.

So let us bask in this embrace,
The radiance of a sacred space.
With every heartbeat, let us sway,
In subtle radiance, come what may.

Frigid Charisma

In winter's grasp, a charm unfolds,
With frosty breath, the heart consoles.
Each crystal flake, a story spun,
Of chilly nights and morning sun.

The air bites sharp, yet spirits lift,
Finding warmth in nature's gift.
A silvery shine on the ground,
Frigid charisma all around.

Bare branches lace the azure skies,
Amidst the cold, the beauty lies.
With every frost, a dream ignites,
In frozen realms, life takes flight.

Snowflakes fall, a gentle dance,
Inviting us to take a chance.
In winter's spell, we find the grace,
Of frigid charm in every space.

So let the chill embrace the heart,
In icy realms, we find our part.
For in the cold, we're brought alive,
Frigid charisma, we shall thrive.

Frost-Kissed Splendor

Upon the dawn, where frost resides,
Nature's canvas, the earth abides.
With jeweled breath, the morning glows,
A splendor wrapped in purest snows.

Each blade of grass, a diamond gleam,
In stillness held, a waking dream.
The world adorned in icy lace,
A touched by frost, a gentle grace.

Branches clutch the weight of white,
While shadows dance in softened light.
The beauty breathes, alive and free,
In frost-kissed splendor, we can see.

As whispers ride the chilly air,
Promises made beyond compare.
With every spark of winter's art,
A warmth ignites within the heart.

So let us cherish moments brief,
In frosted hues, we find relief.
For in this wonder, pure and bright,
Frost-kissed splendor ignites the night.

Gemstone Glimmers

Amidst the earth, beneath the stone,
Life's hidden treasures, brightly shone.
Each gemstone glimmers, bright and bold,
A story of ages, waiting told.

In sapphire blues and emerald greens,
Reflections dance in tranquil scenes.
The ruby's fire, the diamond's grace,
In every facet, a timeless embrace.

They whisper secrets, ancient lore,
Of deep-rooted dreams and hearts that soar.
In every shimmer, a wish we make,
With each bright glimmer, the fears we stake.

Together strong, in unity,
These precious gems, a sight to see.
Through trials faced and paths we roam,
In gemstone glimmers, we find home.

So let us seek the light they share,
In every glint, a moment rare.
With radiant hope, we pave the way,
In gemstone glimmers, come what may.

Milton Keynes UK
Ingram Content Group UK Ltd.
UKHW010232111224
452348UK00011B/701

9 789908 520216